Christopher Davenport

50 / 25

25¢

THE POCKET LIBRARY OF GREAT ART

Plate 1. SELF-PORTRAIT *(detail of color plate 29)*

(DOMENICOS THEOTOCOPOULOS)

EL GRECO

(1541–1614)

text by

JOHN F. MATTHEWS

Lecturer, Brandeis University, Waltham, Mass.

Commentaries by the Editorial Staff

published by HARRY N. ABRAMS, INC., *in association with* POCKET BOOKS, INC., *New York*

FIRST PRINTING

Plate 2. LAOCOÖN *(detail of color plate 28)*

Signature of Domenicos Theotocopoulos, "El Greco"

Three generations ago, the artist presented in this collection had been neglected for centuries. There was a time when histories of art, if they mentioned El Greco at all, merely set him down as a mad Spanish painter who deserved to be ignored.

Within the last hundred years, however, the revolution in art and taste which led to what we now call modern painting, has also led to the rediscovery of

El Greco. Today, this sixteenth-century artist stands at the very apex of world popularity.

But the curious history of Greco's reputation is no more paradoxical than the elements which went into the making of his life. To begin with, this most "Spanish" of painters was not even a Spaniard.

Domenicos Theotocopoulos (nicknamed "the Greek") was born about 1541 on the island of Crete. Formerly an outpost of the ancient Byzantine Empire, Crete had suffered many humiliating invasions; and by El Greco's time, it was the property of Venice. Culturally, however, the island still looked east, toward lost Byzantium (where art and Christianity took the form still seen in Greek and Russian Orthodox churches). Sixteenth-century Cretan painting, for instance, had little in common with the secular and "realistic" art of Renaissance Italy. Instead, it was the Byzantine art of the icon, or holy image—whose object was not to represent life but rather to create religious emotion through severely stylized drawing and design.

This was the tradition in which Theotocopoulos grew up and became a painter. Then, at twenty-five, he turned his back upon it.

About 1566, El Greco went to Venice—a city which had adored and perfected an art of the flesh. He went to work in the studio of Titian, who epitomized a lush neo-paganism we might expect the young icon painter to find objectionable. It was a splendid place to learn the techniques of Renaissance painting, cer-

Plate 3. ASSUMPTION OF THE VIRGIN. *1577*
The Art Institute of Chicago

Plate 4. BURIAL OF COUNT ORGAZ *(detail of color plate 21)*

tainly, but how could El Greco work there?

One possible answer, of course, is that by then Titian had begun to give up concentrating on noblemen and nudes, and was turning to the same religious subject matter with which we identify El Greco. By 1566, the impact of Protestantism had aroused the Catholic world to a new enthusiasm for sanctity and martyrdom. And so, to match the changing social atmosphere, Renaissance art tacked to sail with the rising wind of the Counter Reformation.

At any rate, Theotocopoulos transformed himself into an Italian artist with incredible rapidity. He absorbed Titian's techniques of painting and portraiture; experimented with the daring light-and-shadow contrasts of Bassano; and acquired Tintoretto's skill at dramatic composition. From the latter, too, he learned a unique method of painting from wax or clay models, whose construction apparently took the place of preliminary sketches. Within four years he advanced upon Rome, hailed as a new Venetian master—and seven years later, he left Italy entirely.

Toledo, where El Greco settled in 1577, was one of the prime centers of Spanish Catholicism. Seldom, perhaps, have the energies of a whole city been devoted so fanatically to otherworldly objects. Not only was it a headquarters for the Inquisition, but its population was made up largely of priests and monastics. The resultant atmosphere, though dangerous for heretics, was superbly suited to El Greco's genius.

Soon after his arrival, he was commissioned to do a

Plate 5. THE MARTYRDOM OF SAINT MAURICE. *1580–84*
   The Escorial, Madrid

picture for the priests of the Toledo Cathedral Chapter. When he finished it, the Fathers asked him to make some changes, which he refused; whereupon they tried to avoid paying him, which made him famous. Suing, El Greco won an arbitration which decided, along with the price, that his *Espolio* (plates 15 & 16) was "one of the best pictures ever seen."

From then on, his story had little in common with the familiar romantic nonsense about "starving artists." His work was in constant demand, and handsomely paid for. The result, naturally, was paradox.

In a city devoted to asceticism, El Greco lived for nearly forty years, it is said, "so as to enjoy all pleasures at once." This man, whose paintings deal principally with the miraculous ecstasies of martyrdom and self-imposed suffering, occupied a sprawling twenty-four room apartment, where he even maintained a private orchestra to accompany his meals. And though he was a specialist in pictured piety, it is interesting to note that he may never have bothered to marry the mother of his son.

For a final paradox, it should be remembered that El Greco was in many ways what we should nowadays call a "commercial artist"—painting to please patrons who very often gave him strict instructions as to what each picture was to contain. (See plates 21 & 22.) A commercial artist with this difference, of course: that to every subject he stubbornly brought the special complexity of his own artistic heritage and genius.

Plate 6. THE MARTYRDOM OF SAINT MAURICE *(detail)*

Along with his personal vision, what makes El Greco's work unique *technically* was his ability to fuse the two seemingly antithetical modes of Italy and Byzantium. In Crete he had learned the pictorial discipline of the icon maker. In general, the icon (holy image) strove to convey its message simply and directly, but with a maximum of emotional effect. Accordingly, the icon makers reduced the color and drawing of figures and nature to strong, clear patterns. Such highly stylized designs are believed to have influenced certain of El Greco's conceptions and his ideal of religious expression. In Venice, on the other hand, he had mastered an art which dealt with the representation of *events* and *characters*—a dramatic, realistic art, which attempted, not so much to make you *feel* like a saint, as to *show* you the saint in action against a background of the human world.

Many artists before him had used one or the other of these approaches in art. El Greco, uniquely, did both. His special achievement was to capture the essence of a Spanish generation which held life on earth contemptible in comparison with the promise of eternity—and which yearned to achieve a mystical union with God through self-denial and martyrdom. To accomplish this, El Greco intensified the story-telling canvas of the Renaissance with astonishingly forceful stylized elements from the art of Crete.

The result is neither madness, nor, as some have thought, a miracle. It is simply great painting.

Plate 7. CHRIST BEARING THE CROSS. *About 1593. Prado, Madrid*

Plate 8. HOLY FAMILY (VIRGIN OF THE GOOD MILK)
Detail of color plate 17

COLOR PLATES

PLATE 9

Painted 1577–78

HOLY TRINITY

Prado, Madrid

118⅛ x 70½"

Whatever El Greco's opinion of Michelangelo (at seventy he referred to the Italian as a "good fellow who didn't know how to paint"), his own first work in Spain, exemplified by this painting, shows marked traces of Michelangelo's influence in its conception and composition. Notice, for instance, how everything centers on the powerful figure of the crucified Christ. Quite as much as "the exuberant robustness of the anatomies," this trick of focusing the picture on one dominant element reminds us of Michelangelo and the Renaissance. It is a practice which El Greco eventually tended to abandon, preferring to disperse his main elements toward the edges of the composition rather than inward toward a single center.

Even in his first year in Spain El Greco was obviously a superb artist in his own right—but not yet entirely in what was to become his own style.

PLATE 10

Painted 1586–94

SAINT LOUIS, KING OF FRANCE

The Louvre, Paris

46 x 37⅜"

We usually think of El Greco as an artist who painted sanctity at the peak of intensity. For this reason his conception of the monarch-saint in this painting seems especially curious: a thoughtful, rather awkward man whose crown does not quite fit, and who seems less assured and self-possessed than the page at his side. Paradoxically, too, there is nothing very saintly about this king; his face is a *good* face, but there is nothing here (or anywhere else in the picture, for that matter) which conveys the impression of holiness. The quiet, rather sad dignity of this portrait is derived much more from the king's humanness than from any overwhelming impression of his spirituality.

PLATE 11

Painted about 1590

CHRIST ON THE CROSS

The Louvre, Paris

98½ x 70⅞"

This painting, one of several versions of the subject by El Greco, continues an old custom of including the artist's patrons in a picture of a holy subject. Here the donors—two gentlemen in contemporary Spanish dress —are seen worshipping the figure of the crucified Christ. Their unctuous piety is portrayed just as they probably hoped it would look to the world. But behind the donors there looms a vivid sky, angry, menacing, turbulent—a vast threat to what one critic has called their "showy self-righteousness."

Plate 12. CLEANSING OF THE TEMPLE (*commentary in back of book*)

PLATE 13

Painted about 1597

HOLY FAMILY

Prado, Madrid

$42\frac{1}{8} \times 27\frac{1}{8}''$

At the time El Greco painted the *Holy Family* Toledo was full of distressed and suppliant refugees driven from Greek lands by the Turks. The artist's work seems to reflect this distress, which he must have shared. Indeed, the first years of the seventeenth century were also the first years of El Greco's intensified distortions, increasing the torment and storm in his figures and compositions.

The period and the mood are reflected in this painting. With the tempest approaching, the small family, with the little John the Precursor at the right, is gathered very close together in contemplation and protection of the naked Child.

PLATE 14

Painted 1597–99

SAINT MARTIN AND THE BEGGAR

National Gallery of Art, Washington
(Widener Collection)

$75\frac{1}{8} \times 38\frac{5}{8}''$

The distortion of forms is as old as the history of art.
In El Greco's hands, this expressive device took the
form of an uprushing elongation that twists and con-
torts the body out of all proportion. Here, in the picture of the knightly Saint Martin dividing his cloak
with a naked beggar, notice how lightly the latter's
huge figure rises from the earth—as though the dainty,
almost feminine feet did not so much *support* the
upward thrust as *depend* upon it. It is by such qualities
of the bodily forms—the nobility of the figures, and
especially of the marvelous white horse—more than
by the gestures and facial expressions, that El Greco
conveys the spirituality of the episode.

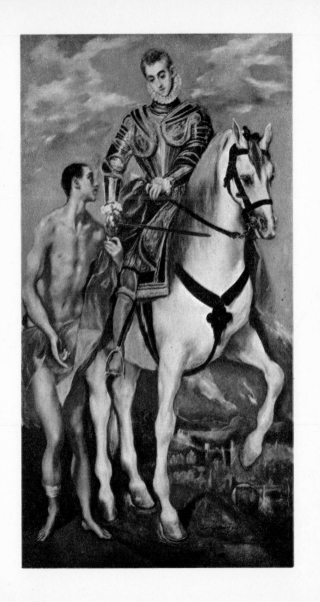

Painted about 1579

EL ESPOLIO

Cathedral, Toledo

112¼ x 68⅛"

This is the picture that made El Greco famous in Spain. It was painted a year or two after his arrival on order from the priests of the Toledo Cathedral Chapter, who commissioned a "despoliation of Christ by the Roman soldiers."

The painting is organized in the Renaissance manner with the main focus on the massive central figure of Christ, or more particularly, on Christ's brilliant garment—at which the fingers of his captors are already grasping. Around this vividly clothed Christ there circles a scheme of independent yet associated figures and heads, each of which leads the eye on around to the next, but inevitably draws the attention back again to the blazing cloak in the center.

lift flap to see detail of this plate

PLATE 17

Painted about 1598

HOLY FAMILY
(VIRGIN OF THE GOOD MILK)

Hospital of San Juan Bautista, Toledo

44⅛ x 41⅜"

El Greco loved to paint mysteries—to seize upon those cryptic moments when the human spirit stands revealed in some relationship with divinity. And it is a mistake to think that for him these were always moments of agony or ecstasy.

Sometimes, as here, the mystery is sweet and serene, for this is a picture of parents, full of the wonder and gentleness of loving adults in the presence of an infant. And the marvel of it is not only in the faces. It is seen even in the fingers of those long, delicately protecting hands, which encircle the child so lightly and with such reverence. One senses here the holiness, not only of this family, but of love itself.

PLATE 18

Painted about 1600

SAINT JEROME AS A CARDINAL

National Gallery, London

23 x 18½"

Here is a picture which illustrates the paradox of El Greco's style. On the one hand it is a vivid and strikingly personal portrait. The earnest, sincerely troubled face of the learned Saint, represented in the uneasy majesty of his scholastic eminence, is a triumph of that penetrating realism of which the Renaissance was so proud. But on the other hand the devices of Byzantine painting are here, too—the symbolic distortion and elongation, the separation of the elements of the story into small compartment-like areas, and the stylized geometry of the composition as a whole.

Yet Greco achieves an awe-inspiring dignity as he unifies these diverse elements, and gives us a portrait in which the subject is conveyed, not merely in terms of an understanding of his character, but also in terms of a suggestion of his significance.

Plate 19. CHRIST ON THE MOUNT OF OLIVES *(commentary in back*

PLATE 20

Painted about 1600

SAINT JOHN THE EVANGELIST

Prado, Madrid

35¼ x 30⅜"

For El Greco's contemporaries the meaning of such a picture as this was to be discovered in terms of its theological significance. In this instance, a saint illustrates the utility of faith by means of a miracle, which, incidentally, confirms the fact that he is truly a saint.

More specifically, the reference is to an apocryphal event in the life of Saint John, whom the Emperor Domitian tried to murder by putting poison in the Sacramental Cup. The poison, however, revealed itself by turning into a serpent. After warning away the Evangelist and his companions, the serpent killed their enemies.

Painted about 1586

BURIAL OF COUNT ORGAZ

Church of Santo Tomé, Toledo

191⅞ x 141¾"

In 1578 El Greco was commissioned by the parish priest of Santo Tomé to paint the story of a miracle: Count Orgaz, a fourteenth-century nobleman of extraordinary piety, was at his death honored by "the descent from open heaven of Saints Stephen and Augustine," who themselves lifted the body and put it in its sepulcher.

For the moment, heaven has opened to earth, but nobody is surprised, or stunned, or even particularly curious. Even the little flickering hands are merely indicating the obvious. Meanwhile, in heaven, everything is active, passionate, dynamic. The embryonic soul of Orgaz mounts through a whirling vortex, pushing up past the Virgin and the company of pleading saints. Everything absent on earth finds expression in heaven.

El Greco called this painting "my sublime work."

lift flap to see detail of this plate

PLATE 23

Painted about 1600

DON FERNANDO NIÑO DE GUEVARA

The Metropolitan Museum of Art, New York

67½ x 42½"

Here, in the magnificent crimson and lace of his ecclesiastical office, sits another of El Greco's remarkable paradoxes, the Cardinal of Toledo and Grand Inquisitor of Catholic Spain. At first glance, the portrait seems merely a splendid and rather shrewd version of what we would *expect* a Grand Inquisitor to look like. But suddenly, unexpectedly, as we notice the mouth the whole face reveals insecurity—as if the Inquisitor himself were accused of something.

The contrast is echoed throughout the picture. One hand is graceful, limp, relaxed, the other is fiercely contorted and grasps the arms of the chair with almost desperate violence. The same violence agitates the folds of the robe on the same side of the picture.

PLATE 24

Painted 1604–09

FRAY HORTENSIO FELIX PARAVICINO

Museum of Fine Arts, Boston

43¼ x 33"

Paravicino, a brilliant poet-scholar of the Trinitarian order, is remembered today chiefly because of his friendship with El Greco, whose genius he celebrated in four of his finest sonnets. And the painter—not in return, necessarily—paid the poet the compliment of this splendid portrait.

For a change, there is nothing paradoxical here. The poet is at ease, and one meets him directly for what he is—a pale, rather passionate man, whose face is illuminated with strength and sensitivity. The hands, widely separated by the soft and flowing folds of the robe, help to bring out his character: the one so graceful and passive, the other embracing the books in a gesture that is close to a caress.

PLATE 25

Painted about 1604

SAINT LUKE

Cathedral, Toledo

38⅝ x 30¾"

According to legend, Saint Luke made the first picture of the Virgin and Child. Later, artists sometimes painted themselves as Saint Luke, using their patron saint as an excuse for self-portraiture.

Is this, then, a picture of El Greco? No one really knows. We do know he painted self-portraits occasionally, and this passionate, slightly cross-eyed, Near-Eastern face appears several times in his work. There is a weary, aging, and ill-looking version of this face in another portrait (plate 29) that most writers think is El Greco, so possibly this is too.

Painted 1597–99

VIRGIN WITH SANTA INES
AND SANTA TECLA

National Gallery of Art, Washington
(Widener Collection)

76⅛ x 40½"

For the mystics the soaring of the spirit is all that truly counts in the universe; even the body joins in yearning upward. This theme runs through El Greco's work with a conviction and assurance that is seldom more magnificently demonstrated than in this picture. See, for instance, how easily and how naturally this lovely Virgin asserts her holiness through the simple elevation of her body in space. Indeed, so skillful and persuasive is the picture that there is not even anything of assertion here; there is merely the elegant statement of fact. The Virgin literally floats upon air.

LINCOLN CENTER FOR THE PERFORMING ARTS
Philharmonic Hall

"K. 458 The Hunt," by the American Sculptor Dmitri Hadzi, cast in bronze, is approximately ten-and-a-half feet high and weighs 1,600 pounds. The title and inspiration for the work were derived from Mozart's Quartet of the same name. The work stands on the Plaza level of Philharmonic Hall.

Manhattan Post Card Pub. Co., Inc., 913 Broadway, N.Y.C., N.Y.

MADE IN
DEXTER PRESS, INC.
WEST NYACK, NEW YORK

© 1966 Lincoln Center for The Performing Arts, Inc.
DT-10690-C

lift flap to see detail of this plate

PLATE 28

Painted about 1606

LAOCOÖN

National Gallery of Art, Washington
(Kress Collection)
55⅞ x 76"

The punishment of Laocoön, a Trojan priest who had offended the gods, is the only pagan theme in El Greco's entire catalogue, and yet it is a theme related in its way to that of the Counter Reformation: the weeding out of the disloyal and dissident. Following the custom of his time Greco gives the ancient story a contemporary setting: the city in the background, toward which the Trojan horse advances, is not Troy but resembles Toledo instead.

Compositionally the whole picture seems to whirl outward from the head of Laocoön. What helps hold this dispersed canvas together are the two sets of upright figures, Apollo and Artemis on the right, and a son of Laocoön on the left. The pervading browns and greens also unify the picture in terms of color.

detail of plate 28 (please lift flap)

PLATE 29

Painted about 1604

SELF-PORTRAIT(?)

The Metropolitan Museum of Art, New York

$23\frac{1}{4} \times 18\frac{1}{4}''$

Most writers on Greco consider this the master's self-portrait. The second inventory of El Greco's effects, made by his son Jorge Manuel and dated August 7, 1621, mentions a portrait of his father which may be the present picture.

The face of this old, sickly, and tired-looking man appears in others of Greco's paintings, particularly in the *Saint Luke* (plate 25). It is remarkable here how the unusual grey tonality of the face—the pigment of an ashy yet luminous texture—expresses the decay, the almost cadaverous decomposition of the flesh.

PLATE 30

Painted 1604–14

TOLEDO

The Metropolitan Museum of Art, New York

47¾ x 42¾"

Never has such a landscape been painted. All the simplest and usual elements of a landscape painting are there: sky, hills, a city, meadows, roads. But the main thing is missing: the feeling of space and distance. Dominant instead is the feeling of activity and drama, a feeling usually conveyed only by the human figure.

The sky is rent in a chaotic rush of clouds, while the earth dashes to meet it in an upward surge. The menacing anger is accumulated behind the zone of Toledo's most conspicuous and haughty buildings: the Cathedral and the Castle, the embodiment of the joint powers of the city, the Church and the State.

PLATE 31

Painted 1605–12

ANNUNCIATION

Collection Oscar B. Cintas, Havana, Cuba

39½ x 26¾"

Although this is a late work, Italian influences are still present. The figures are voluminous and distinct; the angel's dramatic stance is in the grand Venetian manner, as is her superb athletic body; and the drastically foreshortened head of the Virgin is still close in type to those of Tintoretto and Jacopo Bassano. Yet El Greco invests the episode with a spiritual urgency and an ethereal fragility that are wholly personal. A remarkable invention is the dove whose outspread wings delicately link the two pairs of palpitating hands.

Plate 32. THE SAVIOR. *About 1608. Greco Museum, Toledo*

Plate 33.   VIRGIN WITH SANTA INES AND SANTA TECLA
Detail of color plate 26

Plate 34. EL ESPOLIO *(detail of color plate 15)*

Plate 35. AN UNKNOWN MAN. *About 1594. Prado, Madrid*

Plate 36. HEAD OF SAINT FRANCIS. *1592–99*
Hispanic Society of America, New York

Plate 37. HOLY TRINITY (*detail of color plate 9*)

Plate 38. HOLY TRINITY (*detail of color plate 9*)

Plate 39. SAINT JOSEPH AND THE CHILD. *1599—1602*
Museum of San Vincente, Toledo

Plate 40. TOLEDO *(detail of color plate 30)*

Plate 41. RESURRECTION. *About 1600. Prado, Madrid*

Plate 42. ASSUMPTION OF THE VIRGIN. *1608–13*
Museum of San Vincente, Toledo

Painted about 1595

CLEANSING OF THE TEMPLE

National Gallery, London

41½ x 50½"

In this picture we have perhaps the best of El Greco's late versions of a subject which he had originally painted early in his career. Many of its elements reveal his Venetian training. But in contrast to the pomp, the expansiveness, the suavity of his Venetian teachers, there are prominent elements deriving from Byzantine art. Most striking are the marked reduction of depth in the crowd, the bulging oval volume which contains the figure of Christ, the interplay of sharp angles and curves in the drawing of single figures, the continuity of line from figure to figure across the picture. The eye is drawn in conflicting directions by the action, but recognizes the stabilizing effect of the yellows, blues, greens, and greys which reflect and gravitate around the purplish figure of Christ.

Painted 1604–14?

CHRIST ON THE MOUNT OF OLIVES

National Gallery, London

$40\frac{1}{8} \times 52''$

Here is a picture which not only achieves the Renaissance effect of illustrating a story (Christ's Agony on Gethsemane), but also, in the Byzantine fashion, tries to pictorialize an emotional experience. It is, so to speak, a picture of revelation itself. The sleeping disciples in their massy chrysalis of cloud, the angel with the chalice of bitter decision, and the looming threats of sky and rock—all are involved as expressive elements in this moment of climax. Only the tiny band of approaching soldiers is represented as *moving*. Everything else is seized up in Christ's rigid tension—at once isolated and unified through the rhythms and contrasts of shapes and colors.

BIOGRAPHICAL NOTES

1541	Domenicos Theotocopoulos (later called "El Greco") born at Candia, the capital of Crete.
about 1566	Moved to Venice where he studied with Titian, and perhaps also Tintoretto and Bassano.
1570–72	In Rome; forced to leave perhaps because of slighting remarks he made about Michelangelo.
1577	Contracted to paint *Holy Trinity* for Church of Santo Domingo el Antiguo in Toledo.
1578	Son, Jorge Manuel, is born; Greco may never have married Doña Jeronima de las Cuevas, his lifelong companion.
1579	Painted *El Espolio* for the priests of the Toledo Cathedral Chapter.
1580	Commissioned by King Philip II to paint *The Martyrdom of St. Maurice* at the Escorial.
1586	Finished *Burial of Count Orgaz* for the Church of Santo Tomé in Toledo.
1604	Rented twenty-four rooms with gardens and courtyards at the palace of Villena.
1614	Died in Toledo. Inventory of effects listed seventy-two books, little other property.

Recognition of El Greco's greatness has been spectacularly slow. No other great artist was so long ignored and then, in modern times, so lavishly rediscovered. In his lifetime he was showered with honors, perhaps because Counter-Reformation Spain provided a specially prepared audience that could share the ecstasy of his religious visions. When the feverish spirit of the Inquisition died down, so did the appeal of El Greco's violent emotionalism and extravagant individuality. Interest in his work was stimulated after three centuries of neglect by a Spanish scholar, Manuel B. Cossio, in a study published in 1915, and by the writings of the German critic, Julius Meier-Graefe, shortly after. The El Greco boom has also been variously attributed to the growth of nineteenth-century individualism, to a religious revival in France led by Maurice Barrès, another of the pioneer El Greco appreciators, and to the new century's interest in the "primitives" and in the art of Cézanne.

Perhaps the most fascinating commentary on the fluctuations in El Greco appreciation is the history of the sale of the *Portrait of Cardinal Niño de Guevara* (plate 23), a painting privately valued at $200,000.

According to Meier-Graefe, writing in 1915, a value of 25,000 pesetas (about $625) was put on the *Cardinal* when it was found early in this century. Various offers were made for the picture, which was finally bought by a dealer for 200,000 pesetas and was then re-sold to a famous American collector, who later bequeathed it to The Metropolitan Museum of Art.

SOME OTHER BOOKS
ABOUT EL GRECO

Leo Bronstein. *El Greco* (The Library of Great Painters).
New York, Harry N. Abrams, 1950

Manuel B. Cossio. *El Greco*. Barcelona, Hijos de Thomas,
1915 (The pioneer El Greco study, with a complete
catalogue of his work)

Ludwig Goldscheider. *El Greco*. New York, Phaidon,
1949

August L. Mayer, *El Greco*. Munich, Hanfstaengel, 1926

Julius Meier-Graefe. *The Spanish Journey*. New York,
Harcourt, Brace and Co., 1926
(One of the earliest and fullest appreciations of the
artist)

Elizabeth du Gué Trapier. *El Greco*. New York, Hispanic
Society of America, 1925